**Wayne Dyer books' wisdom conc**
# HEAVEN ON EARTH
# PLACE

-

# IT IS A FEELING

Compendium of Dr. Wayne Dyer's 55 most significant tenets of life and more

by Nino Anders

Freiheit. JETZT!
[ Freedom. NOW! ]

# *Preface*

I congratulate to your decision to realize heaven on earth, also in your life.

Dr. Wayne Dyer has been a monumental man, spiritual leader, author and apotheosis of life. His first far spreading, succeeding book was called "Eroneous Zones". It became an outstanding success and starting point of is vibrant career as speaker and author.

With his books, presentations, movies and audio-programs he supported millions of people to make their life easier, more pleasant and financially free. In this book you are about to read his highest and most meaningful tenets of life.

In line with this are the speeches of honour from his daughters Saje, Serena and Skye at his celebration of last fare-well. They are so moving and make clear, what an outstanding life Dr. Wayne Dyer has lead and which heavenly circumstances are possible, when his ideas and believes are put into practice – because what he was able to think and do – we can too.

I wrote this book out of awe about his delighting ideas and way of living. It is actually surprising, that he continues to grow in popularity even after his passing-on. I created this compendium to enable humanity to read about his most significant ideas in a very easy and compact way.

As one of his most prominent recommendations, Wayne Dyer advocated to prime and allow our subconscious mind, which is responsible for 95% percent, to steer our life. Read one of the 55+ tenets every evening before you fall asleep and let the beauty of the ideas sink into your subconsciousness and hence paint your life colourfully.

Enjoy and have fun!

Nino Anders

## Table of Contents

Preface ................................................................ 2
The 55+ most significant thoughts of wisdom by Dr. Wayne Dyer ................................................................ 6
1.- Believe in yourself! ........................................ 7
2.- Give! What you have – and at the same time, what you desire ................................................................ 8
3.- Decide to be benevolent ................................ 9
4.- Be open for new ideas ................................ 10
5.- Take your time and do everything with great patience 11
6.- Trust your imagination ................................ 12
7.- Be grateful for rejections ............................ 13
8.- Do not compare yourself to others .............. 14
9.- Excuses begone! Let go of them all ........... 15
10.- Find happiness within yourself ................. 16
11.- It is your choice to fall in love .................. 18
12.- Disregard your reputation ......................... 20
13.- Follow, what YOU love in life .................. 22
14.- Use the magic of intention ........................ 23
15.- Stop worrying at all! ................................. 24
16.- Do not strive for mediocrity ..................... 25
17.- Change your view upon your ambition .... 26
18.- Cooperation is always better than competition ........ 27
19.- Always think optimistic ............................ 28
20.- Stop judging others! ................................. 29
  1. Valedictory - by his daughter Saje ........... 30
21.- You are part of your surroundings ............ 37
22.- Love and value yourself ............................ 38
23.- Do not wait until the storm has passed – Learn to dance with it ................................................................ 39
24.- Know yourself better ................................. 40
25.- Stop blaming others for their failures ...... 41
26.- Fulfill your dream through having your goal clearly in front of your eyes as already real ............................ 42
27.- Do, what you love the most ...................... 43

28.- Practice Meditation..................................................44
29.- Live your life, without regret................................45
30.- Keep your life in simplicity.................................46
31.- Loose your fear by omitting the word "mistake" from your vocabulary...............................................................47
32.- Read constantly and expand your consciousness.....49
33.- Love people for how they are – and not for how you would like them to be.................................................50
34.- Think of you as a genius! ....................................51
35.- Master the theory of self-actualization.....................52
36.- Behave like water ................................................53
37.- Treat others like you love to be treated ...................54
38.- Discover happiness in the giving and serving others 55
39.- Trust your gut and follow your instincts. ................56
40.- Try to lower your expectations..............................57
   2. Valedictory - by his daughter Skye.........................58
41.- Believe in miracles ..............................................63
42.- Learn to forgive and to forget.................................64
43.- Be willing to take risks ........................................65
44.- Say goodbye to the "I'm not" mentality...................66
45.- Fear and stress exist only in your head....................68
46.- Love your friends as much as your family ...............69
47.- Be who you are....................................................70
48.- If you feel to make a difference, you have to have the courage to change things..............................................71
49.- Watch babies when you have the time ....................72
50.- Truth is something you live..................................74
51.- Act upon your word..............................................75
52.- Don't be greedy, be grateful for what you have. ......76
53.- Do not fear death .................................................77
54.- Diseases develop in the mind ................................78
55.- Use and steer your subconsciousness.....................79
56.- Share!..................................................................81
   3. Valedictory - by his daughter Serena.....................82
   Dr. Wayne Dyer`s best quotes ...................................93
   Outroduction ...........................................................113

Sources ............................................................................ 115
Disclaimer of liability ...................................................... 116

## *The 55+ most significant thoughts of wisdom by Dr. Wayne Dyer*

# 1.- Believe in yourself!

Dr. Wayne Dyer always said that it is important to believe in ourselves. We can be *"beings who create miracles."* Which is only possible, when we think, that it is possible. Miracles occur mainly through inspiring others. Your dreams can come true, in the form of a miracle, when you believe in the possibility of their realization through you.

Usain Bolt does not run the 100 meters in 9.72 seconds if he believes: "No one can do it in less than 10 seconds". But he believes in it, he believes in himself and succeeds.

Miracles occur through people who dared to believe the "impossible" to be possible and making it with persistent thought and action real.

Faith is the origin of the following realization.

## 2.- Give! What you have – and at the same time, what you desire

We reap what we sow. Our life's circumstances are the mirror of our inner attitudes, which we send out with our thoughts, words and actions.

What we send out and therefore give, we attract. We always get more of that what we give. He who thinks and speaks ill-favorably about others is also spoken about alike.

He, who speaks kind and appreciative about others, is also spoken kind and appreciative about.

How do you like people to think and talk about you? Speak and think about others exactly like that.

# 3.- Decide to be benevolent

There is no reason and no necessity to insist on what is "right". All people are entitled to their own opinions and to think their own way. By choosing to be kind and good-natured, you avoid conflict and endless explanations, why you are right.

Deciding to be friendly means accepting people in doing what they do. When you think and act this way, you drive hostilities away and enjoy a more peaceful world.

When you have the choice of being "right" and being "kind", choose to be "kind", and you are always "right". Which is highly encouraging to do, because it is easier to be "right", and more rewarding to be "kind".

# 4.- Be open for new ideas

Ignorance is definitely not a blessing. Life is a constantly changing process. Changes are inevitable. Those who do not expand their knowledge by exploring new possibilities - stagnate. New ideas can improve your life. If certain thoughts and ideas do not improve your way of life, simply let them go.

Never give up searching for new ways to improve your life. Always be open and eager to accept new challenges. Challenges teach you lessons, which help you succeed on your journey and help you to experience what your highest potential is.

Always be embracive about the new.

# 5.- Take your time and do everything with great patience

Try to read this book in five minutes and you will certainly not fully understand it. If you read it slowly and you take the time for each section and to think about the content, Dr. Wayne Dyer's lessons will have a more lasting effect.

Allow yourself the quiet time; your effectiveness and productivity will not be positively affected if you rush through things. It is always about quality, and not quantity. Now you learn to be patient. Patience allows you to be grateful for every step along your path to success and to enjoy the process itself. Through being calm and relaxed, fewer errors and mistakes are made. Endurance and resilience will be improved if you allow yourself enough time.

# 6.- Trust your imagination

Have faith in your dreams. All the developments and technologies we use today were once ideas in the minds of individuals. Ideas are powerful because they are the cornerstones of human development. Phones would not exist today if Alexander Graham Bell did not imagined about a way, how people could talk to each other, in real time, while they are in distant places. It would not be possible to travel by plane today without the creativity and imagination of the Wright brothers.

Make your dreams come true by imagining your ideal outcome as exhilarating and pleasant as possible.

The physical world is based on the realization of the psychic world. In the beginning is the thought, the dream, which is repeatedly thought, spoken about, acted upon and finally realized.

What do you allow to happen in your life?

Plant the seeds of positive thoughts and let them grow and prosper through your focus to fruition.

# 7.- Be grateful for rejections

Dr. Wayne Dyer said that we should also be grateful for the people who said 'no' to us. Rejections can help us to discover how to do things our way. In life, rejections are inevitable. They also tell us that our decisions may not have been ideal. They allow us to recognize initially overlooked opportunities; they show us improvements we can make.

Don't be too hard on yourself in case you are rejected. All people are rejected from time to time anyway. In the future you will know what to do if you encounter a similar situation again.

# 8.- Do not compare yourself to others

God formed us humans uniquely. People do things their own way. Each person has something that others do not have; not all people can do what others can because no two people are exactly the same. Focus only on being the best version of yourself. Set your own rules and standards. He, who always compares himself to others will never be happy and content with what he has achieved. There will always be people who are "better \ different" from you. Try not to be like others, that is not you.

In the same way, others can never be what you are. You have your own way of doing things that are different from other people's ways. Cherish your uniqueness and do, what no one else can do.

# 9.- Excuses begone! Let go of them all

If you like to achieve your goals, then question the thoughts and stories in your head, which told you why you could not achieve something. If you have any doubters, prove them wrong. Be silly enough to believe that you can achieve the impossible. Your confidence disappears as soon as you begin to doubt.

Remember that people who are successful in their field, such as famous soccer players or actors, also have critics. They become successful and impressive because critics point out where they can improve.

# 10.- Find happiness within yourself

Do not desperately search for love. Being in love does not guarantee you perfect bliss. In the same way, being alone does not mean that you must feel lonely or abandoned. Being single allows you to surround yourself with several lovers at the same time. It also enables you to have more time for yourself; to have more time for the things you individually love to do; to concentrate on your career. Besides, happiness is a choice any way.

Do not believe in the concept of the "better half". A person is not incomplete because he or she is single. Those who believe in this concept let other people determine their own happiness. You can not find your other half anywhere else because you already have it, you are already perfect. Take full responsibility for your own happiness.

Happiness is not something we find outside, as advertising or our consumer society tries to persuade us. *"Only when you drive this car you are happy with all the nick-nack"*. Everyone knows that the bubble of happiness bursts faster than the smell of a new car disappears. What you do not see in advertising is that we have the choice every day. It is a conscious decision to be happy or unhappy.


Viktor Frankl lived through the time in a concentration camp. He was happy despite his unfavourable circumstances. He became aware that other people can take a lot from you, but not the control over your own mental attitude. If you decide to be happy every day – about your relentless beating heart, thankful that the sun is shining, that you are able to walk and smell or simply the fact that you are living, which is a miracle itself, then you alone determine your mental health and happiness. When you allow your life to be in pure happiness with your decision, then you experience what it means that:


Heaven on earth is not a place - it is a feeling.

## 11.- It is your choice to fall in love

Just as being happy is your choice, falling in love is your choice. Many people mistakenly believe that a special person will come and give their life what they lack. Dr. Wayne Dyer recommended to be in a constant state of love for everything and everyone. You attract what you are and not what you want.

The idea of wanting something means that you are NOT. This means that you unconsciously keep this away from you. But if you truly love to be in love or happy, then you simply decide NOW to be so - and your circumstances will confirm it.

Just let love flow out of you. When you are in a complete state of love towards everything and everyone, people will automatically emerge, who are interested in a romantic relationship with you. When you are then in a relationship, do not focus on the things you want to receive from your partner. Instead, focus on how you can contribute to their personal growth. Support your partner in fulfilling his/her dreams and finding his/her purpose in life. Let things happen naturally.

## 12.- Disregard your reputation

You can not fully control what other people think about you. Be aware, what others think does not reflect your true character. You will never be happy if you always seek for the approval and recognition of others. It is impossible to please everyone because everyone has different opinions. True self-confidence comes from your faith in the thoughts you think are true about yourself and life. Self-confidence is not measured by how successful you lead your life. It can also never be checked by others. You alone determine the extent of your self-confidence and self-esteem. As a side-note, your success as well. You decide what success means to you and you are automatically successful in your moment of decision. Just give up trying to please everyone or satisfying everyone. Do what you love to do with no worries about others thoughts. Every life is special and unique.

The important people in your life do not bother you and those who bother, are not important for your optimal life. Be courageous enough to stay away from unimportant people. Just let people go their way who think you could not be better and surround yourself with people who make you feel good and help you grow.

# 13.- Follow, what YOU love in life

You will always stay in the same place if you do not take a step forward. Do not waste your potentials. Do not be afraid to remove obstacles. Life is full of challenges that help you grow as a personality. If you never pursue what you really love, you will never get it.

Close your eyes and imagine yourself 80 years from now. After such a long timespan, you will not regret the things you did when you were younger. You will regret the things you have NOT done. And now you have the chance to be young again. Open your eyes and voila! You are young! Fully capable of taking the first step in the virtue you love to pursue.

# 14.- Use the magic of intention

According to Dr. Wayne Dyer, intention is the origin of all things. Every physical object has once been a thought in someone's mind. Who placed this thought in this somebodies mind?

The collective consciousness, life, gave birth to this thought, as much as to the person him- or herself. Everything is intended from the all traversing field.

Start to ask yourself – "Why am I here?" "What is my life about?" "What is my intention and gift to humanity?"

You will receive answers. Simply apply these answers and you walk in your ideal purpose and fulfillment. It is that simple.

## 15.- Stop worrying at all!

It is a waste of time. Worrying does not change the past; nor does it benefit your present and future. It steals your happiness and twists your mind. Whatever the outcome - there is always a second chance. If you worry about anything, you are preventing yourself from fully enjoying the gift of life. Ask yourself, "Will my worries pay my unpaid bills? "Will my worries influence another person's decision in my case?" Give yourself 10 minutes to worry.

Make a list of all the things that concern you. Worry - and see if your "worrying" changes anything on the outcome. No – life happens anyway.

Focus on what can be positive and good - and thus becomes. And if not, see the positive in it, what you learnt from it. Seeing things positively and optimistically is your choice – a tremendously delightful choice.

# 16.- Do not strive for mediocrity

Most people believe that they are normal and average. Their thoughts (product of past influences) tell them that they might not be leading a successful life. Too often they think the thoughts are true and that they have to be better than others. They constantly demand and are never satisfied. Above the thoughts in our mind, resides our soul, which is extensive. The soul is infinite and eternal. If you love to grow holistically and completely, you have to pay more attention to this part of yourself.

Listen to your inner voice, the voice of your soul, the intuition that is the source of omniscient wisdom for you and your life. She knows exactly what the ideal next steps are for you. Practice listening to her and being generous. With generous actions you enrich the lives of others and by following this inner voice naturally, she becomes louder and louder.

# 17.- Change your view upon your ambition

Your ambition is always about you and only about you. It is always about how well you have done something compared to others. It is always about the "I" instead of the "we". Follow your dreams by being an inspiration in the lives of others. The realization of your dreams depends not only on your life, but also on that of the people around you. You cannot achieve your goals without others.

You will not be successful in life if you remain your focus solely on yourself. Your success grows significantly with your ability to support the people around you to succeed. Learn and practice daily to feel grateful for the support of others and more and more support is given to you.

# 18.- Cooperation is always better than competition

If your motivation is to be better than others, then you let these other people control you. The feeling of separation from others only causes more suffering and pain. As mentioned before, help others achieve their dreams. Do not see them as 'tools' that you can use to achieve your selfish goals. Rather, try to experience how you can make a greater vision real together. By 'Taking Action' together you learn new things, you get to know your fellow human beings better and together you achieve more.

In addition, you get to know yourself better because others often give you hints on how you can develop further.

## 19.- Always think optimistic

Think always purely the highest thoughts about others. Forget negativity. Change the way you see things. As Dr. Wayne Dyer said, everything that happens in your life can either be seen as an opportunity to grow or as an obstacle to your growth. It depends on how you see things. See the good in the "bad"; and do not worry about the "negative" experiences of the past, you can not change them anyway.

See the negative circumstances in your life as an opportunity to improve yourself and create new, even greater things.

# 20.- Stop judging others!

Every human has his/her own stories. You do not know where someone has gone through to become who (s)he is today. You also prevent yourself from seeing the good in others by judging them. There is no benefit in seeing yourself standing above others. What you see of others is only a small part of their personality and not what they really are.

> " Never judge another until you have walked in his moccasins for a moon."
>
> - Native American Indian proverb

God, the universe, subconsciousness or whatever you prefer to call it, does not reward those who are good at judging others, but those who are good at enjoying their lives while supporting others. Life is not a competition; it is a cooperation with as many connected fellow human beings as possible.

## 1. Valedictory - by his daughter Saje

After the first twenty tenets of wisdom, the first funeral celebration speech of Wayne Dyer's daughter Saje follows now:

" My father would not have wanted a funeral where we sit sad and cry for him. Nor would he have wanted many people to concern themselves with his death. Death is something he did not believe in, and he often said that he does not "do" funerals. That is why we call today's event a celebration of life and that is why I just want to share some funny memories I have with my father.

There was no boredom with my father. He was the funniest and most entertaining person you could surround yourself with. When he wasn't giving a lively rant against genetically modified food, gun control or coffee enemas, he made everyone laugh with his inappropriate and sometimes perverse jokes. Being around him was addictive and his good mood was contagious. Sometimes I would get up in the morning, put on my fitness clothes and go for a walk, but then I would enter the living room with my father and it would take me hours to get into the aisles.

I still can't really believe he's gone. I am full of pictures of him lying there lifeless and of his last moments. My heart hurts in a way I never thought possible. Tears flow from my eyes because I am filled with the greatest possible feeling of loss I have ever experienced. Even if it is wrong what my mind insists on, what I feel in this chaos and confusion, I am also reminded of many of the ideas that my father taught me and the whole world. I have been so lucky to travel the last 3 weeks with Dad and my sister and her husband through Australia and New Zealand. During this time we laughed so much and grew even closer together. My father insisted on rooms that were connected so that he could enter whenever he wanted. He came to our room every morning and woke us up with his singing: "Oh what a beautiful morning, what a wonderful day. I have an incredibly good feeling, everything falls into my lap," as loud as he could and opened the curtains to let the sun shine in and wake up our eyes. One morning, after finishing his normal wake-up routine, he crawled into my bed, put his head on my shoulder and said, "Let's do a selfie." On other days, he shouted my name out loud while practising one of his famous coffee enemas: "Quajey, I need your help to make my coffee." Just because he knew I would say, "Dad, that's disgusting, I'm not going to help you with your coffee." My father was the light of every room he entered, even in the last weeks of his life.

During our time in Australia I gave a short 20 minute speech to my father's lectures. Before my father called me on stage, he had his own, traumatizing way of presenting me. He told the audience the story of my procreation. His reason for telling this story was to bring the audience closer to the fact that actually everything spoke against me standing here today because he had "withdrawn in the critical moment". As you can imagine, it made me turn a little red in the face and stuttered a little with the words. When he introduced me to the first one, I entered the stage, took the microphone and said, "I told him not to use the word "Withdraw" and what do you know? That's exactly what he said." The second time he introduced me like that, he called me "Withdraw" by saying: "Please welcome my youngest daughter on stage, Withdraw Dyer". It became a kind of running gag between Dad, me and the audience.

His very last message to me two days before he died was:

"I love you "Withdraw". I am so happy that you insisted on coming here. You make the stage shine. This was a journey that none of us will ever forget. I love you infinitely. Dad."

I answered him that I enjoyed the journey too, but my name is not "Withdraw". He replied:

"Withdraw stands for WD. The same initials as your father. On the journey now. Become aware soon."

Besides all the laughs and memories from this trip, I am so grateful to have had the privilege to hear my father talk for 21 hours on 5 different days during these 3 weeks in Australia and New Zealand. I can hear his words so clearly in my head and it gives me so much comfort. On countless possibilities during these 21 hours my father spoke again and again about the beauty of death. He talked about how often he envies those who have already arrived on the side of infinite love. He talked about his new book, which he wrote with Dee Garnes, "Memories from Heaven," which revolves around countless children who shared their experiences of Heaven before they came into this world. He also said that whenever you are confronted with the death of a loved one, you have the choice to overcome your sadness "sooner or later," and he said: *"I tell all people, including myself, to choose sooner."* I also had the good fortune to hear Anita Moorjani speak about her temporary transition into the other, timeless and infinite world, filled with endless, unconditional love. Needless to say, that this has brought about a change in my view of death. My father taught me that we are not our bodies and not our thoughts. There is a part of us that is infinite, that is pure love and that is who we really are. Now that I am still a person with body and mind, I cannot so easily renounce the deepest feeling of sadness in my life. If I can calm down and hold back my sobbing for a moment or two, I feel comforted in an inexplicable way that my father is now part of this infinite world which he has studied and taught so hard.

There are still some funny things about my father that you probably don't know and that I want to share with you.

Whenever any of us were in Maui and he had to leave the city temporarily, which meant that we stayed there without him, he left us the most explicit instructions on how to take care of his plants. Part of that, of course, was when and how we should water them, how much sun they should get, and so on. He also insisted that we should talk to them for at least 10 minutes a day and always wish them good night and love them before going to bed. And I'll tell you something - these were the healthiest plants I've ever seen.

Whenever an ant, mosquito, cockroach, fly, salamander, etc. came into his apartment, which happened quite often, because he usually left the doors open and the air conditioning out, he would stop everyone and say: *"Don't you dare kill that little cattle, he or she is my friend and this is not a funeral home"* and we just had to deal with living with his "friends" in our apartment.

Summarized - My father left this worldly level at a time very unexpected for me. Now that I have recently spent so much time with him again, it seems all the more difficult to me to understand that someone who was so alive and full of joy has now set out on his new adventure. But I knew that his time had come and that he wanted it that way. I will miss him more than I can ever explain, but his teachings live on with us, his 8 children, our children and so on. I love you, Dad, and I know that you are with me forever. In love, your baby, Saje aka "Withdraw".

"If you knew who would walk beside you and accompany you on the path you chose, then you could never experience fear or sorrow." - 'A Course in Miracles' Dad, I know you're going with me and it reassures me so much.

Saje

# 21.- You are part of your surroundings

When you begin to realize that all things are connected in some way, then you begin to see possible growth opportunities in all experiences - good and bad. If you recognize a little bit of yourself in all others, then you no longer have any real enemies. Then you will only feel compassion for those people who wish to harm others. When you begin to recognize yourself in others, you will feel a greater desire to help them. You want the best for yourself and for others.

The good that you initially only wanted for yourself will now extend to all others. Your personal growth is no longer just your own. It is also about helping the people around you to grow.

What we see in others, is our personal focus and therefore the reflection of ourselves. Start to focus purely on the good in others.

## 22.- Love and value yourself

You were made by God. You are God's treasure. If you feel not fully happy and content, remember that there were about 300 million sperm that tried to get on your mother's ovaries first. Only a single sperm managed to fertilize the egg. This is you. If not even you love yourself, who shall? Love yourself first, because you cannot love another person until you learn not to love yourself.

You cannot give what you do not have. If you love yourself, everything else will follow. You will have more self-esteem. You will have more confidence in yourself. These virtues will be realized in you and you automatically inspire others by purely being you.

## 23.- Do not wait until the storm has passed – Learn to dance with it

Life ist not about the waiting for the right opportunities; it is about making the most of every opportunity. Do not wait until the time is right; create the perfect moment yourself. Do not wait for great things to happen. Force them to happen. Do not let unfortunate experiences weaken you. Have the courage to face them.

Psychological studies show that people remember negative experiences more than positive ones, because they draw their attention to dangers they should avoid in the future. Self-preservation is always the most important concern. On the other hand, use adversity as an opportunity to grow. How you react to the "storm", is what makes you a better and happier person. As Dr. Wayne Dyer said, you already have everything for your complete and total happiness. Do what you have to do now.

## 24.- Know yourself better

Know the things you can not.

Sometimes people do not know, that they are allowed and able to ask for and accept the help of others. Recognize your own strengths and weaknesses, which gives you clarity, where you can ask others to help you.

You seek the help of others, because you appreciate learning from them; you reach out to improve. By teaching you the insights of their lives, they also become better - and as already mentioned, life is not a competition, but a togetherness with all dear fellow human beings.

# 25.- Stop blaming others for their failures

It is quite normal for us humans to make mistakes. Accusations however, do not make us happy nor content. You only waste your time accusing others. This time could be used for much more meaningful things.

Accusations only stress, don't change anything for the better and only promote discord. It makes things worse because it destroys the relationship with others. Instead of blaming, you can consider ways to improve the situation.

Always be gentle, kind, empathetically warm-hearted and understanding, with everything you say.

# 26.- Fulfill your dream through having your goal clearly in front of your eyes as already real

Now just imagine yourself as the person you love to be. Learn to train your thinking in the way you would be thinking when you reach your dreams. Do not think about how hard it might be to reach them. Shirkers do not win. You only loose when you stop taking step after steps towards your ideal outcome, no matter how big. Apply the habits of your ideal outcome.

Dr. Wayne Dyer believed that all human beings have unlimited creative possibilities. He said that destiny is under our control. All you have to do is balance your path of life. Depression, stress and anxiety are the reflections of the absence of balance between your dreams and your daily routines.

## 27.- Do, what you love the most

Dr. Wayne Dyer believes that success in life cannot be measured by the balance of your bank account. Rather, it is to do what makes you happy. Follow your heart. Do what you love and love what you do. In this way, abundance automatically flows to you.

We humans naturally tend to do it the easy way. Why do we feel, that there are possible paths seeming easy or difficult? It has been orchestrated by the magnificence of life as a hint and guidance for us to choose. Whichever option feels the easiest and most lucid towards our ideal outcome is highly probable the way to go.

## 28.- Practice Meditation

Increase your awareness of the creative abilities within through daily meditation. Dr. Wayne Dyer meditated every day to realize the love and beauty that was guiding his life and helped him realize his prominent outcomes. Meditation improves your memory and creativity; it improves your attention span. It can also help you fall asleep pleasantly.

One way of meditation is simply to become aware of all things around you: the barking of a dog, the sound of the rain, the silence of a river, through which you appreciate life more and more.

# 29.- Live your life, without regret

It was normal that people viewed decisions unfavourable at times. Remember, you would not be the person you are today, if you did not make the past decisions you made. Let go of what you can not change any way. Forgive yourself and delete the "What ifs...". No more "would have" or "could have" as well. These thoughts prevent you from being happy in the present. An unfavourable decision in the past might have cost you a great chance. Which is no reason for despair, because there will always be a second, third and more chance.

Likewise, there are always more than enough reasons to be grateful. Use every day and enjoy every second of your life. Many do not appreciate things until they loose them. Learn from them, learn to appreciate the things you have and the people around you – who knows where they will be tommorrow.

# 30.- Keep your life in simplicity

Simplify your life by accepting that it might not be perfect. Always wear a laugh and be friendly to the people around you. Get rid of the habit of telling negative things. Eat healthy, conscious and with plenty of raw, living food. Eat to live!

Do not be afraid to show others your feelings. Cry if you feel like crying. It helps you to relieve strong emotions. Spend time with yourself alone without thinking too much. Know your priorities and the things that are important to you. Try to reduce your to-do list and plan in some of your simple pleasures every day. If you pay attention to these simple tricks, you will enjoy life a lot more.

# 31.- Loose your fear by omitting the word "mistake" from your vocabulary

Dr. Wayne Dyer said that the word "fear" stands for "False Evidence Appearing Real". People are afraid because they do not like to make mistakes. However, there are no mistakes, only experiences. The decisive factor is how to deal with the outcomes. Thomas Edison, the inventor of the light bulb, once told reporters that he did not make any mistakes, but only found 10,000 ways how something did not work. Michael Jordan's famous quote goes in line:

*"In my career, I missed 9,000 baskets. I lost over 300 games. 26 times I was given the ball to throw the winning basket. I tried over and over and over again, often times I failed. But that is the secret of my success."*

You grow through your mistakes and get to know the things and ways that do not work. Over time you get better and better and success is guaranteed – as long as you keep going.

# 32.- Read constantly and expand your consciousness

Read books if you have the time. Build up a stock of knowledge, because it can be very useful in possible future emergency situations. Practical side effects are increased analytical thinking, increased vocabulary, increased concentration and improved creativity. Long-term studies show that constant reading prevents or at least delays Alzheimer's and senility due to increased brain activity. Your brain appreciates training to be fully functional. Reading is an excellent way to realize your potential potential.

Choose your influences and information very consciously. Books are a much better source of information than newspapers or TV. Try to avoid the mass media, because they have a negative influence on your way of thinking. Do you really have to thave a TV? Does the truth really stand in the daily newspaper or in the New York Times?

# 33.- Love people for how they are – and not for how you would like them to be

You love people not only for their great abilities, but also for their small imperfections. If you really love someone, do not try to change them. Do not love him for what you hope or plan, how he should be; do not try to turn her life upside down so that it suits you, you will only satisfy your ego. You do not marry someone because you hope that he or she will change. You marry someone because you love the person the way he or she is and how he or she makes you feel.

Also remember this by thinking about yourself. Life is about how we make others feel. And you and everyone else is special, unique and precious in their own ability of feeling for humanity.

## 34.- Think of you as a genius!

That does not necessarily have to be a public announcement. Still, remember yourself again and again that you are a masterpiece, the crown of creation; a human being, born for a higher destiny. You never have to prove it. You can only know inside yourself that you are and have a unique gift to offer to the world. In this way you avoid having to apologize for yourself.

We are free to think, believe and feel about ourselves what we prefer. Always remember:

*"The world tends to accept the way we think and feel about ourselves."*

## 35.- Master the theory of self-actualization

Self-actualization is the thrive to reach your highest potential; it is the desire to become what you may become. Decrease solving problems outside yourself, look inside first and take pleasure in improving the lives of others as inspiration. Be spontaneous with your thoughts, be open and unconventional.

To master self-actualization, take your time to explore your own potential. Draw inspiration and fulfillment from simple experiences. Every moment is a fantastic experience that you can enjoy and appreciate. Self-actualized people value the path as much as the actual successes.

## 36.- Behave like water

Water takes on the shape of its container. It also creates many other possibilities, such as swimming, surfing, diving, drinking and others when it simply flows. Do things, of course and definitely, then you also create opportunities for others.

Be there. Show up. Keep your word with your actions. Do what it takes relentlessly. Persistent and gentle. Soft and soothing, definite in its assured success. Do whatever it takes in a friendly pure manner, then you are like water.

# 37.- Treat others like you love to be treated

Always apply this golden rule. It goes far deeper than just being friendly to others. It is sometimes about creating equality and adjusting your views. Do not see yourself as someone better; always be humble and considerate of the feelings of others. Always pay attention to honesty and good intentions behind your actions. Make it easy for other people to love you and you will be rewarded for it.

> *"We reap what we sow. What we shout into the forest, is what resounds. What goes around, comes around."*

Trust these eternal proverbs of wisdom and what the elders always knew.

# 38.- Discover happiness in the giving and serving others

Support is one of the learned virtues of Lao Tzu - giving and serving without expecting anything in return. Let spiritual fulfillment and joy be your reward. Serving others gives you the altruistic feeling of being part of their lives. People will remember that you have helped them and will help you in times when you appreciate help.

And even if it is not the exact person you helped, it comes back in the face of another. Always do as much as you can for others and you will be rewarded, that is assured.

# 39.- Trust your gut and follow your instincts.

Refer to the integrity of your mind; listen to your inner signals because they help you make better decisions. Our mind has the ability to feel and anticipate coming dangers. If you feel it is wrong, do not ignore it.

Our body is a wonderful invention with so much wisdom in every part. Every part and signal is there for a reason and appreciation for it is welcome. Listen and trust to what is inside of you, it guides you on your individual ideal path.

# 40.- Try to lower your expectations

Researchers at a London university have proven that lower expectations make us happier, because there is a good chance that the result will exceed our expectations. There is hardly any sense of disappointment if these low expectations are not met.

On the other hand, high expectations often lead to frustration because they are less likely to be achieved. Think according to the motto: "Have big dreams, with low expectations."

==Be happy with simplicity== and see every exceeding luxury as a gift.

## 2. Valedictory - by his daughter Skye

Now it is time for the speech of his second daughter Skye.

" Hello to everyone. Thank you for being here to celebrate my father.

I had the luck to travel with my father over the last 13 years and sing at all his events. I have never taken for granted the time I could spend with him. My father asked, when I was 21, if I wanted to go on tour with him. At that time, I was going through a change in my life and Dad helped me find my new way. My father was my biggest fan. He saw something in me and wanted me to believe in my talent, but also that it was not mine alone, but that I was just a vessel through which God's gift could be realized. I always loved this idea. Dad wrote me *"I am brave"* on a piece of paper and wanted me to carry it with me at all times. It helped me when I was singing, because I became so brave on stage, but also in real life. My father lived his life fearlessly, he knew his purpose early in his life and I could understand that so well. It was magical to see him on stage, he was the greatest teacher. He was here to teach us all love, because love is the only thing that counts.

My family has already said many things that we will miss with him. There are so many and everyone has shared so impressively what life with him looked like. I will miss, how funny he was. He was so fast; when a joke had to be told, he was the first. He loved telling jokes and telling the same ones again and again. I loved that about him, it was the cutest quality of all. My favourite joke was: *"Why can't witches get pregnant on Halloween? Because goblins have invisible weenies."* He told us this joke when we were little kids and we didn't understand it, but when we figured out what it meant, there was no stopping.

He was happy about the smallest things and it was a pleasure to watch his face when something so small meant so much to him. That's something I admired extremely about him, that he was always enthusiastic and saw miracles everywhere. I will miss his spirit, his wonderful spirit. I have learned so much from him and will continue to grow as a spiritual being because of him. He would recommend books for us to read and would know the answer to almost everything he was asked, it was incredible. I heard him talk a thousand times and it never got boring. He had this gift of being able to explain ideas and answer life's big questions. His memory was extraordinary, how a person can store so much old knowledge and share his own knowledge was supernatural for me. He was a real gift to our world.

What I will miss the most, is his unconditional love for me and all my brothers and sisters. I have always felt loved, never condemned or belittled, he made us all feel special. Fortunately I got the gift of having him as a father. He enlightened every room he entered. He loved that I sang and always talked about it. When I sang on stage, I felt indestructible because he stood there with me, full of pride. I am so grateful that I never let my ego get in my way, sometimes I thought of a career of my own, but now I know why I never stopped.

My father was love and he often told me that I was the definition of love, but I think I learned that from him before I was even born. He always said that we choose who our parents are before we come into this life. I feel so happy that I decided to spend this life with him and I will always be grateful that he decided to live with me.

Dad, I am so sad that I am no longer your travel Buddy and we can no longer talk about our plans. I will miss so many things, my mind can't grasp them all yet. Nobody can fill this void, but I know you're here. I will continue to choose kindness over right. I will continue to love unconditionally. Most of all, I will continue to love you and be your loving daughter.

I would like to close with one of my father's favourite poems about the death of Emily Dickinson:

*"This quiet dust was gentlemen and ladies*
*And lads and girls;*
*Was laughter and ability and sighing,*
*And frocks and curls;*

*This passive place a summer's nimble mansion,*
*Where bloom and bees*
*Fulfilled their oriental circuit,*
*Then ceased like these."*

I love you, Dad, always and forever.

Skye

## 41.- Believe in miracles

The universe works in mysterious ways. Dr. Wayne Dyer always said that he believes in miracles. The fact that you exist at this moment is a miracle. What Dr. Wayne Dyer meant is not hoping for abnormal or inexplicable events, but small gifts like a raise or a new fruitful friendship. It is about to always believe that something good is going to happen; having a positive attitude to life.

Miracles are everywhere.

# 42.- Learn to forgive and to forget

Forgiveness allows you to release the resentment, anger and bitterness that some used carry within themselves. This exercise frees from the things that weakened us and prevent from continuing with life. Moreover, we only hurt ourselves when our thoughts are about revenge. Mahatma Ghandi said:

> *"Forgiveness is the ability of the strong. Be a strong personality and not a victim of the whims of others."*

Always be forgiving, not for anyone else, but for yourself. You like to free and feel pure pleasant feelings, for that reason, let go of anything unpleasant. You can forgive verbally or in person, it can also be simply an mental exercise in your mind. Let go and be pure.

## 43.- Be willing to take risks

Do not be afraid to take risks because you can not really loose. As mentioned earlier, we only create results. If at some point your performance does not achieve the results you anticipate, do not hesitate to try again or something else.

We only grow through taking that next step.

# 44.- Say goodbye to the "I'm not" mentality

As a student with a worse grade than your classmates, you might have thought, *"I'm not smart."* Similarly, if a boy or girl you really liked, did not like you back, you might have thought, *"I'm not attractive."* To overcome this negative mentality, you have to trust yourself. Try to replace the words with which you define yourself. Instead of, *"I'm not good enough to be accepted,"* tell yourself, *"I'm good enough."* Make yourself aware that your reality, the life you live, is the exact reflection of your inner attitudes. And these inner attitudes are boundless and 100% under your control, because you decide what you think, what you feel and therefore what manifests in your life. In that way, your ideas become your reality. You are, whatever you define yourself to be. Let go of the old believes, which do not serve you any more, which might have taken on subconsciously. When you notice them, become aware of them, and exchange them to new, encouraging believes.

In practice – write a list. Pin a blank white paper on your fridge and whenever you become aware of one, write the encouraging statement on your list.

# 45.- Fear and stress exist only in your head.

It is you alone who creates these false attitudes. Many people commit themselves to stressful thinking. Dr. Wayne Dyer believed that perceived fear and stress is only caused by false images of the ego. Stress is hardly caused by external forces. It is mainly caused by the belief that you have to win and be better than others, or what by commitments, where others force you to do things, which you do not feel like.

Stress is the manifestation of the imbalance between your dreams and your daily habits. Do not allow your ego to dominate your life and reconcile your daily habits with your dreams. In this way, you free yourself from stress and fear. Live every day as if it were your last and turn your daily routines into enjoyable activities.

If this means to quit your current job, do it. There is an opulence of other businesses around. Switch your focus to discover and explore other option, the doors will open. What we focus our attention on, expands.

# 46.- Love your friends as much as your family

Sometimes there are things, only your friends can understand. Celebrate the moments you share with them. Be grateful for them because they are there when you appreciate someone to listen to you. Acknowledge the little things they do for you.

Respect and cherish the friendships you have. You can actively reach out to create them consciously. We often times set goals to reach this in business or run that fast in sport. Still, also other areas of our life can be actively pursuit. You find friends at events or areas of your highest interest and your both strong interest in one particular area makes you feel aligned. Embrace everyone for this, because not everyone shares what you love predominantly.

## 47.- Be who you are

There is a reason for everything. Dr. Wayne Dyer's philosophy is to realize, that we are not what we own. The dilemma by identifying with possession is, that if they disappear, your identity disappears with them.

According to Dr. Wayne Dyer, the only purpose of life is to be happy and to reach the point where you do not strive to be anything else.

It is about being who you are, being fully happy and content with yourself, with the things you do, give and your life.

## 48.- If you feel to make a difference, you have to have the courage to change things.

Dr. Wayne Dyer thought it necessary to leave the herd to make a difference. Be innovative. Have the courage to question the status quo and find your own ways to master challenges. In the animated film *"Paranorman"*, a boy named Norman Babcock managed to bring peace to the community by speaking to the company that caused the threat. Nobody else dared to do that before, except him. Get up and make a difference and you improve the lives of many others.

There is a good reason why you have the thoughts and feelings you have. Take Action on them, the most courageous are doing so. Be courageous.

# 49.- Watch babies when you have the time

Dr. Wayne Dyer liked to watch babies because they have no other motivation but to discover the world around them. They are in a constant state of love and bewilderment. You can see that babies are happy even if they do nothing. Babies love everyone and are easy to please. They are completely thrilled by a grimace or a plastic toy. This is because they are in tune with the source that brought them here. They have no resistance to bliss, no *"reasons"* to be happy, like a car or a payraise, they simply are. Be like a baby you once were and you will go happier through life.

At the same time, not only the elder are our teachers, also the young. There is so much we can learn from babies, how they relentlessly push and push to do this very ever first step. To turn over from the back to the front; to sit upright. They never did it, yet they see that it is possible and there is no one to explain them how to do it, they simply learn it themselves by trying, trying, trying, until it is done. What wonderful analogy to a business for example.

No one of us came into this world and being able of doing business. Everything is learnt and as babies finally learn to walk, we are finally able to successfully do business, as long as keep at it. By the way, business is only a word reflecting your own unique passions fruitfully monetized.

## 50.- Truth is something you live

Be honest with yourself and stay true to yourself, everything else will follow. Honesty is always the best basic rule. By staying true to yourself, you avoid the frustrations that can arise from living according to other peoples' plans. Avoid excuses; they prevent you from accepting and progressing with your individual imperfections. Remember, you are unique, also because of your imperfections. Accept them and use them to develop yourself. In this way you will be able to make better decisions. Do not judge your life according to the expectations of others. Be honest with yourself and everyone else. Your life is simply so much more pleasant that way, because, remember, how you treat others, is how you are treated by others. Be honest and allow others to be honest to you.

# 51.- Act upon your word

Your true character is shown through your actions. You are not really honest with yourself if you do not act according to your words. Do not be a hypocrite. Do not pretend to be someone you are not.

Be careful with your definite commitments because it is highly highly beneficial, to always keep your word. And show up in the situations you committed to show up.

Other people are less inspired by the words you say; others are inspired by the actions you take. Inspire by example. Live the truth you are preaching with encouraged actions. Make things happen because life is about 'Taking Action!'

## 52.- Don't be greedy, be grateful for what you have.

If you are not satisfied with what you possess today, you will never be satisfied with anything in your life, because our ego always demands more. Learn gratitude and satisfaction with what you already have. When you die, it will not be possible to take your possessions with you to the grave. Material things will mean nothing when you die. Only your legacy will be remembered. As Dr. Wayne Dyer said, your happiness comes mainly from touching the lives of others. In this way you enrich your soul and bring yourself closer to the creative intention that created you.

Many acknowledged their gratitude as the turning point of their life. Once they started to be grateful and developed a serious appreciation for everything they had and had become, life blossomed exponentially for them. Develop gratitude for every single person in your life. As example, pin on your smartphone-background:

"I AM SERIOUSLY GRATEFUL FOR EVERY PERSON IN MY LIFE".

## 53.- Do not fear death

Through his contact with Anita Moorjani and her account of her near-death experience, Dr. Wayne Dyer learned a lot about the process of dying. Under no circumstances can a hen be forced to lay more eggs, but we humans would give everything and promise not to be mistreated or killed. The nature of the ego to worry about the future offers little added value. But by threatening future worse living conditions we humans let ourselves be enslaved in the system of capitalism.

Death itself is nothing to fear. We return to a place of unconditional love and realize in which illusion we have lived and how we have let ourselves be unplugged from the truth. What we leave behind is not our body, but the ideas we pursued and the difference we have made with our life.

# 54.- Diseases develop in the mind

Also through the influence of Anita Moorjani, Dr. Wayne Dyer learnt a lot about the nature of diseases. He firmly believed that everyone is responsible for diseases, as well as their healing. At first, repetitive unhealthy thoughts like *"I do not feel good"* occur. This is then reinforced by the "confirmation" of a doctor saying "Yes, you have that and that". Now many become more and more convinced that they were ill and try everything to find out what they can do or not do about it. I can not eat this any more; I can not do that any more.

On the other hand, we have the great potential to let everything we love become our reality. This is why it is so elementary to make yourself clear again and again, to convince yourself and simply to know that you are perfect health. Dr. Wayne Dyer did this several times a day. After he was diagnosed with leukemia by a doctor, he lived for more than 2 years without any medication, even if the doctors thought this was impossible. He did not die of the consequences of leukaemia, which his family members made clear based on the medical death results.

# 55.- Use and steer your subconsciousness

Researchers repeatedly confirm that only 3 to 5% of our lives are consciously controlled. At least 95% of our thoughts, actions and attitudes are steered by the subconscious. These imprints originate from our childhood and all experiences of our previous lives. Only two thirds of the day we experience consciously, during the third third we sleep and are unconscious. This offers a great potential to positively program the subconscious.

There are two simple ways to do this. The first possibility is that in the phases of the day when the gates of the subconscious are wide open, to influence it with positive thoughts. Every morning after waking up and especially every evening before falling asleep, bring yourself into a positive optimistic attitude. It makes an extreme difference, if you go in the evening before falling asleep through your shortcomings or experiences of the day that went wrong, or whether you are grateful, happy about what went well. You can also think about what it feels like when the goal you have in mind finally became reality.

A second possibility is to influence your subconscious during sleep, because it perceives your surroundings very well during sleep. If you now play over night quietly, positive affirmations and suggestions, then you may not perceive them consciously, but subconsciously for sure.

The 528 Hz frequency, which is called *"the healing sound"* or *"miracle love tone"*, is also very helpful. Use these tools to uplift yourself.

# 56.- Share!

In his book "Wishes Fullfilled" Dr. Wayne Dyer writes about a hypnosis session in which he was put back into a previous life. Without expecting too much, his words, which were recorded and of which he was completely unconscious, were remarkable. He was transported to a prehistoric time in which cruelties were the normal way people were treated. His mother was killed, he had to leave his sister dying and he saw his son's mother only for a short time before he had to set off on a boat trip while his love was being killed. He became aware, through this kind of inspiration, that all the cruelties of the world are due to man's selfish aspirations. This is the root of all evil. He received the higher truth that anyone who accumulates posessions, hoards it and does not share, will lose them sooner or later. The one who shares comes easily and constantly to prosperity and wealth. This is to be seen as a law. The one who shares supports the universe where he can. He who thinks only of himself loses everything. Tony Robbins also says it so beautifully:

*"The secret of life lies in giving."*

# 3. Valedictory - by his daughter Serena

Here is the third speech, by his daughter Serena:

(Especially revealing when one recalls the 26th principle: *"Fulfill your dreams by having your goal in mind from the beginning"*).

" My father did not use a filter, so my coming description is also unfiltered. I would like to share with you some experiences that you probably don't know unless you have been one of his children or close friends.

There are 2 things for which my father was particularly known, on the one hand his sense of humor and on the other hand his desire to share, be it knowledge, money, stories... He shared and taught at all times with everyone around him.

It was summer, we were on Maui and I was 8 years old. Our family and friends took a catamaran to Molokai Island, where we swam, ate lunch, climbed trees, swam with lianas and jumped into a big pit full of mud and were bled with mud from head to toe. Some of the little children ran around naked and my brother Sands asked my father if he would like to run around naked. My father replied that he couldn't run around naked in the mud for 3 reasons: First, if he did, all the women would go crazy over his peeper (family word for penis) and chase him all over the island. Second, all the kids would think his peeper was a liana and try to swing him around. And third, his peeper would drag on the floor and he wouldn't want him to hurt himself. We all burst out laughing unrestrained and rejoiced heavenly back then, as we do now, 20 years later, about his answer.

My father was very funny, really funny, and whenever we were together we laughed and told stories. My father rarely had simple and short answers to any questions. Just a few weeks ago we took Sailor's pacifier and let it dangle in front of her face so that she could grab it herself with her fingers. Father lay there and watched her and said: *"It's like the legend of Sisiphus, every time she comes closer, you pack it further away"*. With no idea what he meant, he continued to explain the Greek mythology of Sisiphus before breakfast! He always told us stories and taught us, his children.

He was very creative with his stories, he had his own language and brought the punch line like no other. He was obsessed with not wasting things. He never wanted to throw things away and that's why his fridge was always full of expired things. He somehow always noticed it when Skye and I searched the fridge for old products. Then he flew up and said, *"Mustard has no expiration date! I don't care if the label says it will expire in 2009, it's fine and won't be thrown away"*. He used a single sheet of kitchen paper as a plate for his toast every morning for a whole summer, just to prove that it was possible. One sheet of kitchen roll for a whole summer!

However, he and technology had a cruel relationship. He could never really figure out how to use his tablet and always called me and said something like *"Google won't let me youtube my website"* or *"I want to send someone my website by email, how can I give him the password"*. The first time he saw one of us enter a password in front of the PC, he grinned mischievously and said, *"I know your password!"* And we all like, *"Oh, Dad, what's it like?"* And completely serious and convinced, he said: *"Four stars."*

I was shopping with Matt and Dad called twice in quick succession, which meant a technological emergency. For the next 30 minutes, while Matt was in the dressing room, I tried to explain to him how to copy and paste a website into an email and then send it to someone. Other people in the dressing room laughed their bellies at the casual listening to my remarks...

One summer we began to hang some pictures on the kitchen wall. When we came back next summer, the pictures had already spread to other walls and there were even more until Christmas. The strange thing about it was that these pictures were not only of our family or friends, but also of complete strangers. We asked: *"Dad, who is this child?"* And he replied: *"No idea. His mother sent me this picture, so I hung it up."* His apartment in Maui was completely covered with pictures of family, friends and complete strangers. Obviously he had a love for all people.

My father had an inner desire for justice, a desire to do the right thing, even though it was easier to simply ignore certain things. He was just so good, so loving, and he did all those things without the attention for himself, I want to share a few examples with you.

A few weeks ago he saw a show on HBO about a 61 year old African American woman named Harriett Cleveland. She raised her 3 year old handicapped grandson alone in Montgomery. She was financially unable to pay a speeding fine in addition to food and medication, so she put this bill in the stack of unpaid bills to deal with later. However, this penalty grew from $75 to $3000. She was arrested at home, in front of her grandson and imprisoned for 2 weeks. Dad saw her story and was so moved that he asked his assistant to locate the woman, write to her and send her $3,000 for the punishment. In addition, he wrote her 2 more letters with checks for several thousand dollars to make sure she was all right. The woman called him in tears because she couldn't believe that a complete stranger had just sent her as much money as she had never had in her life. Her story was broadcast and only one person, one person in the whole world, did something to help her without any need for attention. That one person was my father.

He received hundreds of letters every week. In some letters people asked for financial support or advice. At the same time, however, letters came from strangers who simply sent him money. People who believed in the principle of tenship (giving 10% of income) sent him incredible sums of money. So when someone asked him for financial support, he simply reached into the pile of letters with money and sent it to the person seeking help. He maintained a constant flow of financial support from complete strangers simply because he could.

He paid for the education of dozens of children without any reference to them, children of friends or strangers, simply because he believed in the value of a good education and he could make it possible. He set up a million dollar fund at his school for children who have trouble paying for school. To date, 74 children have benefited from this fund.

Whenever we walked on Maui together, which was actually the case every day when I was there, he was constantly approached on the street by people who thanked him for how his work had changed their lives. And every time he gave that person the feeling that at that moment she was the most important person in his life. Then he would ask about her hotel and have some signed books sent to her room. This happened regularly. Daily, really.

His stage was incredibly powerful. He attracted huge audiences all over the world and he knew what an enormous impact it had on the careers of individuals who performed with him. Every year, without exception, he involved someone or their story he believed in, in his program. He supported the work of others and in a collaboration he left every dollar of profit to the other person.

Strange as it may sound, I had a desire to be close to my father. I wanted to talk to him, hear his voice and he was always the person I wanted to be most like. Incredibly generous, friendly, interested in the world and people in particular, funny. For his birthday this year, I sent him a card with the inscription that he can be so proud of the fact that his children want to spend all their free time with him, to be around him and that this is the sign of a great man and an even greater father. He called me after receiving the card and said that he loved the card. He loved that his children always wanted to be around him. I am so grateful that he knew how much I wanted to be around him.

My father and I made several trips around the world together, just the two of us, and on one of those trips I wrote him a letter about how much I loved him. He read the letter at each of his subsequent lectures and my sister Skye even composed a song from it which she sang at my wedding and we all danced to it. I am so grateful to have this memory. In this letter I wrote that I felt how he believed in me and what greater gift can a parent give you than to make you feel that you believe in them so much?

When we came up with the idea of writing a book together, a book about how I was raised and how it felt to grow up in the Dyer household, I felt excited but also intimidated. I wasn't sure if I could adequately reflect what it felt like to have him as a father in only 10 chapters. But he was so encouraging, so loving. He worked with me and told me over and over again, *"Serena, you have the gift of telling stories, just tell your stories and it will be perfect."* When we finally wrote the book together, we were both very proud of ourselves. I felt his pride and love for me. I am so grateful that he was the type of father who shared that. I am so grateful that he taught me to go inside me and find God. Grateful that he taught me to be open to the way of life and ideas of others. He taught me to leave judging to others and to meet all people with compassion and understanding, because everyone acts in the way that seems best to him. Most importantly, at this moment, I am so grateful that he taught me that even when we die, we only lose our cloak and put on a new one. He told me that he would never leave me, not even when he leaves the worldly sphere and I am grateful that I know this as true.

Everyone who knows me knows that I am a narrator. My father was also a narrator. Talking to him was my favourite activity in the world. I think that is what makes all this so difficult for me. Our relationship was based on talking to each other. We talked on the phone almost every day. We talked so much with each other that it is so incredibly difficult for me to describe on so few lines who my father is to me.

To conclude, my father and I agreed to call our book *"Don't die with your music still in you"* because this was his most important lesson he taught me. Dad came here with his music and played it so loud that it changed the world. My father with his love for teaching, sharing, telling stories helped millions of people improve their lives. It is now my promise to you, Dad, that I will not die while my music is still on. I carry you with me and I will do everything I can to spread your message, as you asked me recently. For me this is not goodbye. I could never say goodbye to the person who is everywhere and everything for me. For me it's just learning to see and hear you in a different way, as you said, when you die you'll just be in a different room. I love you forever and ever, Dad.


Thanks for everything.


I AM


Serena

## *Dr. Wayne Dyer's best quotes*

Finally, here are the important quotes by Dr. Wayne Dyer compiled, which round off his teachings once again.

*"How other people treat you is their karma; how you react to it is yours."*

*"Change the way you look at things and the things you look at change."*

*"Friends are God's excuse for your family."*

*"You can either feel sorry for everything that has happened to you or see it as a gift. Everything you can either see as a way to grow or as an obstacle that keeps you from growing. You can choose".*

*"When you judge others, you don't define them, you define yourself."*

*"You can't be lonely if you love the person you are alone with."*

*"You didn't get stuck anywhere unless you decide to."*

*"Passion is the feeling that shows you: That's the right thing to do! Nothing can stand in your way. It doesn't matter what others say. This feeling is so good that it cannot be ignored. I will follow my purpose and always act with joy."*

*"Any accusation is a waste of time. It doesn't matter how wrong you feel, what someone else does and how much you blame him for it, it won't change you. Accusations only take the focus away from you when you are looking for external reasons for your frustration or depression. You may be able to make others feel guilty for what you accuse them of, but in this way you will not be able to change why you feel unhappy."*

*"Your reputation is in the hands of others. That's your reputation, you can't control it. The only thing you can control is your character."*

*"If you have a choice between being kind or being right, always choose what brings peace."*

*"I am realistic - I expect miracles."*

*"You already have everything for total peace and total bliss, right now."*

*"The more you already see yourself as what you want to become and behave as if it were already reality, the more the infinite forces that help you make your dream come true, support you."*

*"Conflicts cannot survive without your participation."*

*"Circumstances don't make a man, they reveal him."*

*"You will see it when you believe it."*

*"If you know whoever walks with you, on all the chosen paths, you will no longer feel fear or worry,"*

*"Heaven on earth is not a place, it is a decision."*

*(Author: I changed his quote for copyright reasons and also due to the fact, that life is about the feeling we are living in. Decisions pave the way into a greater and greater feeling. We are it, when we feel like it, after we decided for it.)*

*"You don't have to be better than anyone, just better than you were yesterday."*

*"Begin to see yourself as a soul with a body and not as a body with a soul."*

*"In every relationship in which two people
the end result is two half peop*




*"Your children will understand you more by the way
you live than by the things you say."*




*"Loving people live in a loving world; hostile people
live in a hostile world; the same world."*




*"You are not dancing to get to a certain place on the
floor. You dance to enjoy every step."*

*"You can't always control everything that happens around you. But you can always control what happens inside you."*

*"We are not human beings in search of a spiritual experience. We are spiritual beings having a human experience."*

*"Every experience in your life was absolutely necessary to get you there, to get you there, to the present moment."*

*"Feel miserable. Or motivate yourself. No matter what happens, it's always your decision."*

*"When you rest in peace and love yourself, then it is really impossible to do self-destructive things.*

*"Before saying anything, listen to your innermost truth barometer and resist the temptation to tell people only what they want to hear."*

*"I would rather be hated for who I am instead of being loved for who I am not.*

*"Act now! The future is not certain to anyone."*

*"The highest form of ignorance is when you reject something you know nothing about."*

*"I am grateful for all those who said "no". It was only because of them that I did it myself."*

*"There is no lack of opportunities to make a living from things you love. There's only a lack of determination to do it."*

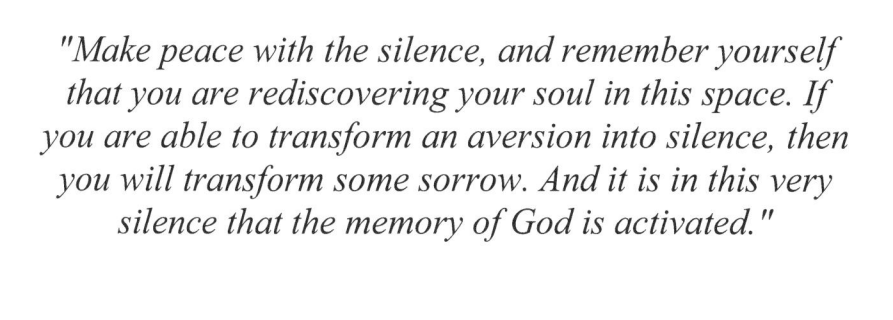

*"Make peace with the silence, and remember yourself that you are rediscovering your soul in this space. If you are able to transform an aversion into silence, then you will transform some sorrow. And it is in this very silence that the memory of God is activated."*

*"You leave behind old habits with this thought: "I release myself from the necessity of what is in my life".*

*"Your circumstances are nothing but the reflection of your thoughts."*

*"You are in a partnership with all other human beings, it is not a competition with being judged better or worse by others."*

*"You'll hardly blame yourself for anything you've done. It is the things you have not done that you regret. The message is clear: Do it! Develop a devotion to the momentary moment. Grab every second of your life and enjoy it."*

*"What comes out of you when you're squeezed is what's inside of you."*

*"Doing that which you love is a cornerstone of abundance in your life."*

*"If you are able to devote your inner attention to serving others, and if you make this the central focus in your life, then you will be in a position of knowing that true miracles will happen on your way to prosperity."*

*"As we focus on what is ugly, we draw more ugliness into our thought world, our emotional world and finally into our sensory world, the "reality"."*

*"If you avoid making decisions, you enter the wide world of excuses."*

*"It is easy to love people when they smell good, but sometimes they dive into the dung of life and smell terrible. You must love them just as much, even if they stink."*

*"Every accusation is a waste of time. No matter how many friction points you find with others, it won't change you."*

*"If you're willing to do more than you have to do, you'll never have competition."*

*"Everything you need now is already there."*

*"Living in the now, contacting your present is the heart of an effective life. If you seriously think about it, then there is no other moment in which you live. The now is all there is, the future is just another now when it comes in."*

*"You will be treated in life the way you teach people to treat you.*

*"Peace is the result of retraining your mind to live life as it is and not what you think it should be.*

*"You are today what you choose to be today. Not what you have chosen in the past".*

*"Don't die while your music is still on."*

*"As soon as you believe in yourself and see your soul as divine and precious, you are automatically transformed into a being who believes in miracles."*

*"Enjoy the silence because meditation is the only way to get in touch with your origin."*

*"Begin with the end before your eyes. Begin with the goal in mind and work your way back to make your dream possible."*

*"A peaceful mind, not focused on hurting others, is stronger than any physical force in the universe."*

*"Nobody knows enough to be a pessimist."*

*"As you think, so shall you be."*

*"I have no limits whatsoever what I want to create."*

*"When you meet someone whose soul is hardly like yours, send him love and go on."*

*"Never underestimate your power to change yourself; never overestimate your power to change others."*

*"Love what you do; Do what you love."*

All quotes are by Dr. Wayne Dyer.

## Outroduction

Thank you again for your choice to read this book.

I hope you enjoyed the combination of Dr. Wayne Dyer's essential life teachings. I am sure you read something new here or remembered wisdom of the elders.

As suggested at the beginning, a repetitive reminder of these life teachings is recommended, so that you can use these positive and transformative basic assumptions in your life.

I recommend you to print the 10 to 15 most important headline-statements for you on an A4-page and hang them in a place you see every day. That way you keep these beautiful thoughts alive daily and live according to these maxims, whereby you, your life and your environment are positively enriched.

Please, as stated in rule number 24, I like to ask for your help. It has such a tremendous effect, when you review this book online. It feels so good to me, that my efforts in creating this compendium are being recognized and appreciated. It also enables others to feel attracted to read these beautiful words of wisdom, which certainly can inspirit so profoundly. Every word of you is appreciated, your favourite and most delighting idea as an "one-liner" is enough. I am eternally grateful for you and your action, we are together in this beautiful life.

I wish you with all my heart that you reach your goals in life and that happiness and satisfaction is your omnipresent companion.

Thank you very much and all the best!

Nino Anders

# Sources

All of (Dr.) Wayne Dyer's books, especially "Wishes Fullfilled" - My personal favorite book by him.

His speeches available on Youtube

Facebook page of Dr. Wayne Dyer

# Disclaimer of liability

You are welcome to share this book with as many people as possible. Talk about it, remember the teachings daily and enjoy your great life :)

The cover was created with the help of the picture of theaucitron - clouds on https://www.flickr.com/photos/theaucitron/5810163712/in/photostream/
Copyright © 2017 Freiheit. JETZT!

All rights reserved. -   ISBN-13: **9781075547973**

**Impressum**

Nino Anders
Papyrus Autoren-Club
R.O.M. Logicware GmbH
Pettenkoferstr. 16-18
10247 Berlin

# Also published by Freiheit. JETZT!: (Freedom.NOW!)

Sascha Të Light & Nino Anders

*Wayne Dyer, Elon Musk, Dalai Lama, Albert Einstein, Bruce Lee, Buddha, Khalil Gibran, Nikola Tesla, Robert Kiyosaki, Dolores Cannon, Jesus Christ, Justin Bieber and more* share their wisdom:
Pearls of the Genius

Hardcover: 14.99 USD
Paperback: 8.99 USD
Kindle eBook: 2.99 USD

This book is a dynamic collection of ideas, which are enriching your life comprehensively. Imagine, you could bring your life easy and precise with the greatest ideas of the greatest minds of human history to fruition. Which circumstances become possible?

Live your life in copiousness Now! thanks to your reading of this book.

*"Nothing is as strong as an idea whose time has come."*

Amazon page: https://amzn.to/3nByJTU

(Also available in German: 'Perlen der Genies'; Italian: 'Perle dei Geni' and Spanish: 'Perlas de Genios')

Sascha Të Light - **How To Be Rich And Free Now** - Apply Just 5 Simple Eternal Money Generating Essentials

Paperback: 7.99 Euro
Kindle eBook: 2.99 Euro

There are basic principles, the 5 Simple Eternal Money Generating Essentials, which guarantee the amassment of wealth when one adheres to them. This precise quintessence presents them to enable every dear reader exuberant profits and freedom. Financial freedom is available to all of us, claim yours now.

Amazon page:
https://www.amazon.de/dp/1656907410

Printed in Great Britain
by Amazon